TO THE LIMIT
IN-LINE SKATING

Martin Smith

PowerKiDS
press.
New York

Published in 2012 by the Rosen Publishing Group Inc.
29 East 21st Street, New York, NY 10010

First Edition

Produced for Wayland by Roger Coote Publishing,
Gissing's Farm, Fressingfield, Eye, Suffolk IP21 5SH
Project Management: Mason Editorial Services
Designer: Tim Mayer

Photographs: The publishers would like to thank the following for giving their permission for photos to be used in this book:
Cover Jamie Squire/getty Images Sport/Getty Images; page14, 15, 20, 21(b), 22, 23(b) 25 Joe Coyne - Editor of Kingdom
Magazine; all other sphotos supplied by Ben Roberts, p. 22 Purestock/Getty Images

Library of Congress Cataloging-in-Publication Data

Smith, Martin.
 In-line skating / by Martin Smith. – 1st ed.
     p. cm. – (To the limit)
 Includes index.
 ISBN 978-1-4488-7026-4 (library binding) – ISBN 978-1-4488-7060-8 (pbk.) – ISBN 978-1-4488-7061-5 (6-pack)
 1. In-line skating–Juvenile literature. I. Title.
 GV859.73.S656 2012
 796.21–dc23
                                    2011028824

Manufactured in Malaysia
CPSIA Compliance Information: Batch #WW2102PK: For Further Information contact Rosen Publishing, New York, New York at 1-800-237-9932

CONTENTS

WHAT IS BLADING? 4

HISTORY 6

EQUIPMENT 8

BASIC TECHNIQUES 12

AGGRESSIVE SKATING 14

GETTING AIR 16

SKATE PARKS 18

COMPETITIONS 20

STREET SKATING 22

PIONEERS AND HEROES................24

ROLLER HOCKEY......................26

ETHICS AND QUIZ....................28

GLOSSARY 30

FURTHER INFORMATION 31

INDEX.............................32

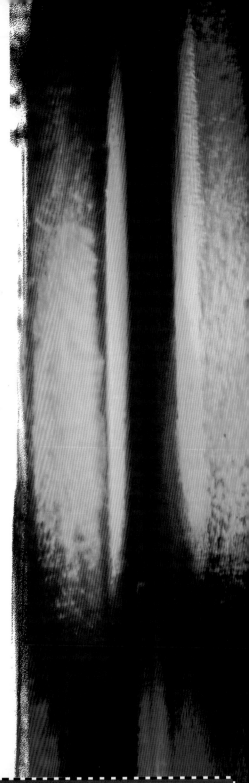

Warning!

Blading is a dangerous sport. This book is full of advice, but reading it won't keep you safe. Take responsibility for your own safety. You should always wear a helmet when doing any kind of in-line skating. In some of the photos in this book, you may see trained professional skaters without helmets on. Don't follow their example! Always keep yourself safe while skating and wear a helmet.

WHAT IS BLADING?

When you first get a pair of blades, the front door of your home becomes a doorway to another world. You will never see your surroundings in the same way again. Your first wobble on a pair of blades starts you on a quest to find the smoothest routes through the streets. Soon you're sweeping downhill or pulling radical airs.

Most people start blading with a gentle cruise around the park on a borrowed or rented pair of blades. But once you've mastered the basic blading skills you'll find your pulse rate and your speed rising.

Blading Tech Talk

Hard boots — Similar in design to a ski boot, gives lots of support (good for beginners).

Soft boots — Boots made from soft sneaker-like materials, advantages are that they're breathable, light, and nice to look at.

Frame — The part of the skate where the wheels are held.

Bearings — Tiny metal balls inside the wheels that help them roll faster.

ABEC rating — Manufacturers give bearings a number to indicate how accurately they are made (higher number means more accurate, faster bearing).

Foot bed — Soft foam sheet that can be placed under the foot; installing a better one is the easiest way to improve any skate.

Bladers enjoying the sunshine.

The Four Kinds of Blading:

- **Recreational:** blading for fitness and fun.

- **Aggressive/street:** performing tricks and jumps on obstacles in skate parks or the street.

- **Hockey:** like ice hockey but on blades.

- **Speed:** blading as fast as you can downhill.

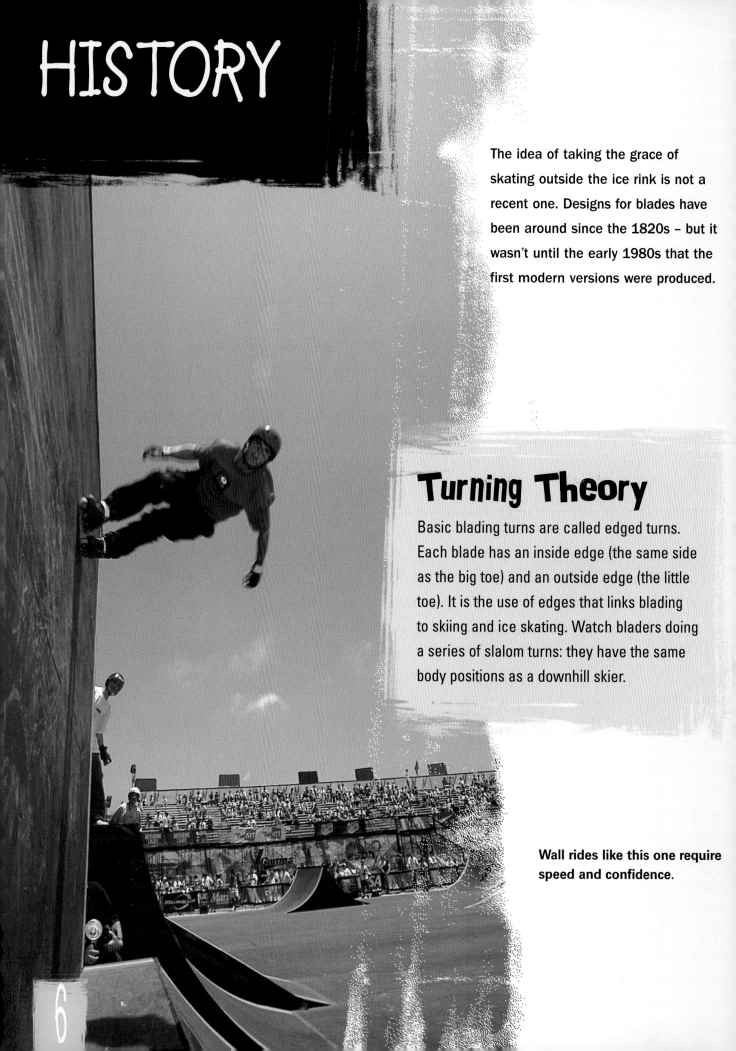

HISTORY

The idea of taking the grace of skating outside the ice rink is not a recent one. Designs for blades have been around since the 1820s – but it wasn't until the early 1980s that the first modern versions were produced.

Turning Theory

Basic blading turns are called edged turns. Each blade has an inside edge (the same side as the big toe) and an outside edge (the little toe). It is the use of edges that links blading to skiing and ice skating. Watch bladers doing a series of slalom turns: they have the same body positions as a downhill skier.

Wall rides like this one require speed and confidence.

Above: Bladers building their own miniramp.

Scott and Brennan Olson, two ice hockey players from Minnesota, used the boots, a rigid chassis, and urethane wheels from hockey skates to make the first-ever blades. Before long, people all over the United States realized that wide, smooth walkways, particularly those of the coastal towns, were ideal places to blade. Skiers, ice skaters, and hockey players appreciated the chance to do a similar sport outdoors in the summer sunshine. Other people caught on too, and soon blading spread to Europe and beyond.

Rough Riders

Early blades manufactured by people like Robert John Tyres were not hugely popular, probably because they had iron wheels!

EQUIPMENT

Each style of blading makes different demands on equipment. Recreational bladers want to be able to wear skates for hours on end. Hockey bladers want to turn sharply. Aggressive and street bladers need grind area. Some skates allow you to cross from one style of blading to another. But it is important to get the right skate for the type of skating you do most often.

Recreational blades

High cuff gives good ankle support. - - - - -

Clip closure for easy fitting. - - - - -

Inner boot thickly padded for comfort. - - - - - -

Perforated boots are cool and light. - - - - - -

Big wheels for higher speed. - - - - -

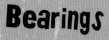

Bearings

Bearings have a major effect on performance. Always get the best bearings you can afford. High-quality bearings cost more but they last longer and are faster. Also, look after your bearings – remember, water and bearings do not mix. Take off your skates if it starts to rain.

Aggressive skate

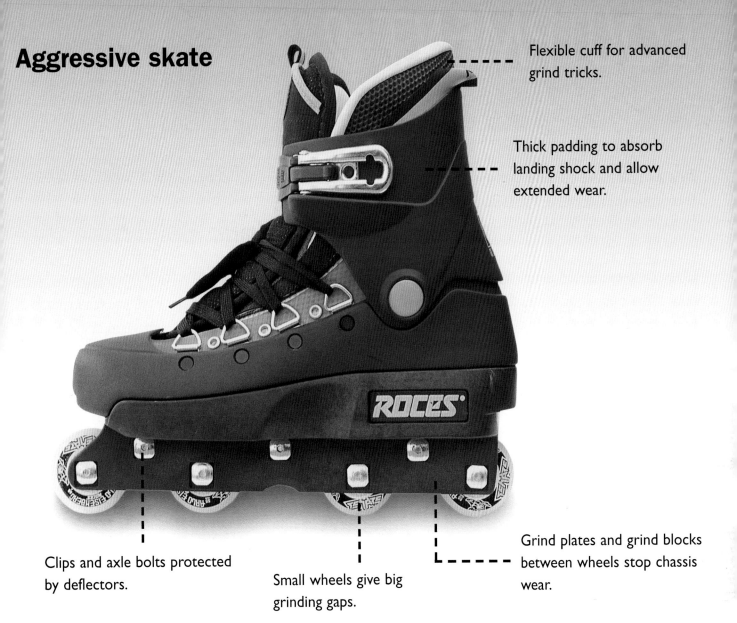

Flexible cuff for advanced grind tricks.

Thick padding to absorb landing shock and allow extended wear.

Clips and axle bolts protected by deflectors.

Small wheels give big grinding gaps.

Grind plates and grind blocks between wheels stop chassis wear.

Hockey Skates

Low cuff allows flexibility for turning; mid-sized, soft wheels for sharp turns and good grip; less padding gives more accurate edge control; lace closure allows tighter fitting.

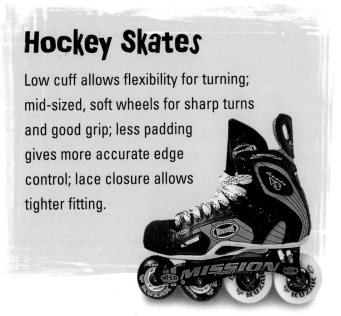

Speed Skates

Ultra low cuff allows extended stride length; fifth wheel for extreme speed; lightweight, rigid chassis minimizes power loss due to flex; lace closure allows tight fit.

EQUIPMENT 2

Safety equipment is important for bladers. The amount of padding you wear should always reflect the worst-case scenario for the type of skating that you are doing. Even the most experienced bladers take a fall once in a while. Remember, when things go wrong on skates, they go wrong very quickly.

Standard helmet

Knee pad

Elbow pad

Wrist guards

Goalie's mask for hockey

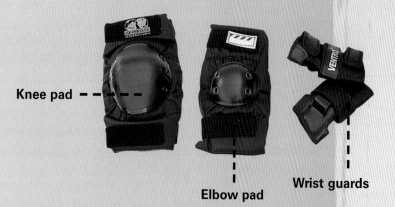

Wrist guards

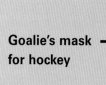

Minimum Requirements

Recreational blading

Wrists guards and knee pads (beginners should add elbow pads, too). Always wear a helmet.

Aggressive blading

Wrist guards; knee and elbow pads are much thicker than recreational pads, to protect you if you fall from high up; helmet. Perhaps shin guards and a pair of padded shorts.

Hockey

Wrist, knee, and elbow pads are the minimum. Hockey clubs will insist that bladers wear full protection during a game – upper and lower body armor, padded gloves, a face visor, and mouth guard.

Speed skating

The need to keep an aerodynamic shape means that padding is kept to a minimum. Wrist guards and a helmet are an essential requirement, but with just these an accident can be very dangerous.

Protection Guidelines

- No amount of protection is too much.
- Think about the skating that you will be doing, and imagine the type of accident that you may have.
- Get fully padded up before practicing new moves.

11

BASIC TECHNIQUES

Brake control is the hardest basic blading skill to learn. Your body's natural reaction when things start to go wrong is to tense up. This causes your knees to straighten and your head to pull back, which is the opposite of good braking technique. So, the first rule is to stay calm.

All beginner blades have a heel brake: this is a large rubber block at the back of one blade. There is more than one way to stop, but heel braking is the first method to learn because it's the easiest. More advanced ways of stopping, like the T-stop and the power slide, require advanced skills.

Heel braking

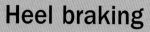

1

Slide the braking foot out in front of the supporting blade.

2

Lift your toe. When the brake is touching the ground, bend your knees. The weight of your hips slows you down.

3

4

Keep everything – knees, shoulders, and head – forward. Stretching your arms straight out in front will bring even more weight forward.

Try to keep the braking foot out in front. If you let it slip back alongside your supporting foot, you will not stop.

Top Tip

If you are worried about putting blades on for the very first time, try walking on a carpet with them on. You won't roll on a carpet and you'll be able to walk around and get a feel for the weight of the blades. When you feel confident, move outside.

The power slide braking technique needs a lot of balance and good edge control. Practice blading on one foot and backwards to obtain the skills needed.

13

AGGRESSIVE SKATING

You don't have to be aggressive to be an aggressive skater! But aggressive bladers do have a different attitude to their sport. To experienced aggressive bladers, the urban environment is an adventure park, full of wild rides. Stairs, rails, curbs, and benches are not obstacles but opportunities for tricks and grinds.

The move that sets aggressive blading apart from all other styles is the grind. Grinds can be performed on curbs, benches, handrails – anything that will slide on a part of the skate. Remember, though: if it's hard enough to grind, it's hard enough to hurt. When learning aggressive skating, it's especially important to wear a helmet, because the back of your head is very exposed if you fall backwards.

Albert Hooi holds a unity grind in Weymouth, England.

Grind Terms

Alley-oop — Any grind performed backwards.

Backside — Turn 90 degrees to the left.

Backslide — Grinding on the edge of your back foot while grabbing the front foot.

Frontside grind — With the rail on your right, turn 90 degrees to the right when you jump onto it.

Sole grind — Front foot across the rail, rear foot in line with the rail sliding on the outside sole of the boot.

Unity — Feet crossed as you slide down the rail.

Empty parking garages are a skaters' playground. Tom Penfound backslides this ledge in Manchester, England.

GETTING AIR

Jumping, or "getting air," is a basic skill that all aggressive bladers need to master. To start with, you will get air when you jump on and off a grind rail, but leaving the ground is only the start of getting air. Spins, flips, and grabs give extra style to tricks, and in competitions big, stylish airs score more points.

How to Air

1 Place the ramp somewhere with plenty of space. Start by rolling up to the ramp very slowly and turning on the ramp. Roll out facing back the way you came.

2 Next, roll in with enough speed to take you up to the lip and roll out backwards (fakie). These moves will familiarize you with the feel of the ramp.

3 Skate to the ramp with plenty of speed and "pop" up as you reach the lip. "Popping" means straightening your knees and is basically a small jump.

4 Bend your knees and keep your weight forward for the landing. Roll out from the landing.

5 Look out for obstacles like lampposts: you may be travelling quite fast!

16

Big Air

The official world record for getting air on blades is 8.9 feet (2.7 m), by Raphael Sandoz of Switzerland.

SKATE PARKS

The skate park is the safest place to learn aggressive skating, meet other people who are into the same kind of skating, and see new maneuvers.

Trick Terms

Fakie — Any trick done backwards.

Grab — Holding skates during a trick.

Bio — A sideways spin performed while horizontal.

Mute — Grabbing the opposite skate with your arm going across the front of your body.

Late — Tricks performed closer to landing, which score higher in competition and get more respect.

When you first enter a skate park, it seems like complete chaos. There are people grinding and pulling airs all over the place. But, there is order in the disorder and it pays to hang back for a while to see what is going on. Our Park Life Rules (right) will help you figure it out.

Miniramp

A smaller version of the vert ramp, usually about 6 feet (2 m) high and definitely the place to start.

Street course

Usually the largest area of the park. Around the edge are hips, quarter pipes, and roll-ins. In the middle are fun boxes and rails.

Vert ramp

The big half pipe can be anywhere from 8 to 15 feet (2.4-4.5 m) top to bottom; not for the faint hearted.

COMPETITIONS

Aggressive skate competitions are fun for bladers of all abilities. Competitors see them as a chance to find out how good they really are. For spectators, competitions are places to meet old friends and keep up with the latest tricks and fashions. For sponsors, they are the perfect places to have their products seen and identified with success.

What to Expect at a Competition:

1 Turn up and register. You will be given a number.

2 Your number will be called with about 20 other bladers for a 20-minute street-skating practice session.

3 When everyone has practiced, qualifying runs will be held.

4 Those who qualify will then skate two runs of 1 minute each in the final.

5 After the street competition has finished, there will probably be a miniramp comp and a vert comp.

6 All the scores are counted and a winner is announced for each section. The winners are showered with prizes and products from sponsors.

Our Top Five Blading Heroes

- Arlo Eisenberg (USA)
- Jon Julio (USA)
- Chris Edwards (USA)
- Chris Haffey (USA)
- Rene Hulgreen (Denmark)

Getting a sponsor

Doing well in competitions is the best way to attract a sponsor's attention but not the only way. Getting along with other bladers and practicing hard are other ways to attract the interest of sponsors. It's not just big manufacturers who sponsor bladers; your local skate shop might also be a source of sponsorship.

STREET SKATING

An empty park on a beautiful summer day is a great place to practice your tricks.

Street skating is the original form of aggressive blading. Indoor skate parks are good places to hold competitions and to use blades when it's raining, but some bladers are never seen there. These are the hard-core street skaters.

As well as the skills needed to do "sick" tricks, street bladers also have to deal with problems like bad weather, traffic, and the general public. There are no judges to please; the pleasures of street skating are pure fun and the respect of other bladers.

5 All-Time Classic Blading DvDs

- *The Hoax 2*
- *E2F*
- *VG3*
- *Damaged Goods*
- *The Adventures of Mr. Mooseknuckle*

Street Survival Kit

Things to have in your backpack:

- Some antiseptic bandages.

- Shoes and, if possible, a mobile phone.

- Plenty of fluid, especially if the sun is out or it's hot.

- A couple of spare bearings: if a bearing disintegrates while you are out, it can ruin a session.

- A blade tool. These combine Allen keys, bearing pushers, and any number of other useful tools.

- Some money for the bus, train, or a cab. If you take a big slam, you might not feel like skating home.

Rawlinson Rivera is striking a pose blading at night.

PIONEERS AND HEROES

Arlo Eisenberg

Even though he was one of the pioneers of aggressive blading in the 1980s, Arlo still skates at a high level.

Arlo Eisenberg

One of the all-time great pioneers of aggressive skating is Arlo Eisenberg. He and Chris Edwards were among the very first people to skate in a style that had more to do with skateboarding than ice skating. Arlo adapted his skates so that he could perform grinds and was one of the first bladers to be into jumps and airs.

Chris Edwards

Chris Edwards started blading when he was 13. At first he skated near his home in Escondido, California, but was soon signed up to skate for Team Rollerblade. "I just wanted someone else to ride with," he says. The first in-line competitions were anything but competitive – Chris won them all. He excels on the big half pipe; at his best, he amazed judges with his massive, contorted airs. Having once said, "I will skate forever," he is still regularly placed in the top ten at competitions.

Jon Julio

Jon Julio has been inspiring generations of bladers since 1995. He has invented countless tricks like the unity, backslide, and topside acid. Along with a successful pro career, Jon's been involved with clothing companies, wheel manufacturers, and he has even founded the street competition, IMYTA. Jon continues to push the sport with innovative videos and his own skate brand.

One of blading's founding fathers, Jon Julio, is still innovating with tricks like this vertical top acid stall to fakie in Manchester, England.

ROLLER HOCKEY

Blades were born out of the ice hockey scene, so it is no surprise that hockey is still part of the sport of blading. The rules of the game are based on ice hockey, with a few adjustments. Any blader with a basic knowledge of how to skate can play hockey. Two of the all-time greats of the NHL, Wayne Gretzky and Brett Hull, promoted blading as an accompaniment to playing ice hockey.

A fully padded roller hockey player.

Club Hockey Rules

- Mandatory protection: helmet, elbow pads, gloves, knee pads, shin guards, and mouth guard. Goalkeepers require extra protection.

- No charging, tripping, or roughing.

- No holding on to feet, hands, or sticks.

- No interfering with a player who doesn't have the puck.

Pucks

Glove

Stick

Standard helmet (goalie's helmet shown on page 10)

Knee and shin guard

Chest and shoulder padding

Basic Street Hockey Requirements

- Normal recreational skating equipment (see page 8).

- One stick per player.

- A crushed soda can to use as a puck if you don't have a ball.

ETHICS AND QUIZ

Blading is a fun sport, and it should be carried out with a smile. When skating around other people, remember that the reason that there are relatively few rules to follow is because everyone tries to get along with each other. Give everyone around you the respect that they deserve. As you become more experienced, remember how you felt when you were a beginner and try to give a little help to people who are just taking up the sport.

You are blading behind a crowd of pedestrians, do you?

A: Shout so that they move out of your way.

B: Push them gently to one side.

C: Slow down and follow behind until you can pass safely.

While blading, you find yourself at the top of a hill that is much steeper than you can deal with. Do you?

A: Keep going and figure out what to do later.

B: Stop and put on more protection.

C: Stop and remove your skates.

You see a beginner having problems, do you?

A: Stop and laugh.

B: Turn up your music.

C: Stop and give some advice.

How did you do?

Mostly A: You should consider taking up meditation rather than blading.

Mostly B: You have the right idea but you should work on your interpersonal skills.

Mostly C: You will be an asset to the blading scene – blade in peace.

GLOSSARY

air (EHR) A jump performed on blades.

bearings (BER-ingz) Tiny metal balls that allow wheels to spin more freely.

cruise (KROOZ) Gentle blading session, taking your time to get from one place to the next.

edged (EJD) Describes a turn that uses the edges of the wheels.

fakie (FAY-kee) Describes any trick done while moving/rolling backward.

grind (GRYND) A trick in which the frame of the blade is used to slide along a wall's corner or a handrail, for example.

half pipe (HAF PYP) A large, steep, double-sided ramp on which bladers (and skateboarders and BMXers) perform tricks.

heel brake (HEEL BRAYK) A block of soft, rubbery plastic on the heel of a blade, which allows bladers to slow down.

power slide (PO-ur SLYD) An advanced braking technique (see page 13 for a photo).

t-stop (TEE-stawp) An advanced braking technique, in which the blader drags his or her foot sideways to slow down.

FURTHER INFORMATION

Books

Crossingham, John. *Extreme In-Line Skating*. New York: Crabtree Publishing, 2003.

Weil, Anne. *Agressive In-Line Skating*. Mankato, MN: Capstone Press, 2004.

Web Sites

Due to the changing nature of Internet links, PowerKids Press has developed an online list of Web sites related to the subject of this book. This site is updated regularly. Please use this link to access the list:
www.powerkidslinks.com/limit/skating/

INDEX

A

aggressive blading 5, 14–15

    equipment 9, 10

air 16–17

    basic technique 17

B

bearings 4, 8

braking 12, 13

C

competitions 20–21

    sponsorship 21

F

frame 4

G

grinds 14–15

    names 15

H

hard boots 4, 8, 9

hockey

    blade hockey 5, 9, 1
26–27

    ice hockey 7

R

recreational blading 5

    equipment 8, 10

S

safety equipment 10

skate parks 18–19

soft boots 4

speed skating 5, 9, 10,

street blading 5

T

turning 6